Low-Fodmap Meal Prep Cookbook

300 Delicious, Gut-Friendly Recipes for a Happy Tummy(4-Weekly Plan for IBS Relief)

Migen Burkey

© Copyright 2021 Migen Burkey - All Rights Reserved.

In no way is it legal to reproduce, duplicate, or transmit any part of this document by either electronic means or in printed format. Recording of this publication is strictly prohibited, and any storage of this material is not allowed unless with written permission from the publisher. All rights reserved.

The information provided herein is stated to be truthful and consistent, in that any liability, regarding inattention or otherwise, by any usage or abuse of any policies, processes, or directions contained within is the solitary and complete responsibility of the recipient reader. Under no circumstances will any legal liability or blame be held against the publisher for any reparation, damages, or monetary loss due to the information herein, either directly or indirectly.

Respective authors own all copyrights not held by the publisher.

Legal Notice:

This book is copyright protected. This is only for personal use. You cannot amend, distribute, sell, use, quote or paraphrase any part of the content within this book without the consent of the author or copyright owner. Legal action will be pursued if this is breached.

Disclaimer Notice:

Please note the information contained within this document is for educational and entertainment purposes only. Every attempt has been made to provide accurate, up-to-date and reliable, complete information. No warranties of any kind are expressed or implied. Readers acknowledge that the author is not engaging in the rendering of legal, financial, medical or professional advice.

By reading this document, the reader agrees that under no circumstances are we responsible for any losses, direct or indirect, which are incurred as a result of the use of information contained within this document, including, but not limited to, errors, omissions, or inaccuracies.

Table of Contents

Introduction 5
Chapter 1: Overview of Low-Fodmap Diet 6
    Key to a Healthy Gut 6
    Low Fodmap Diet as a Lifestyle 6
    What Causes IBS and Digestive Disorders 7
    Low Fodmap Diet Targets & Benefits 8
    List of Ingredients to Avoid 9
    Best Tips to Succeed In the Kitchen With Low Fodmap Diet 10
    Positive Vibes from the Author 11
Chapter 2: Overview of Meal Prep 12
    What is Meal Prepping? 12
    Benefits of Meal Prepping 12
    Tips for Success 12
Chapter 3: Breakfast 15
    Breakfast Popsicle 15
    Cottage Cheese Pancake 16
    Pumpkin Oatmeal 17
    Broccoli & Tofu Scramble 18
    Baked Spinach & Cottage Cheese 19
    Baked Eggs with Broccoli 20
    Breakfast Strawberry Wrap 21
    Breakfast Enchilada 22
    Breakfast Sandwich 23
    Egg Muffin 24

Chapter 4: Soup 25
    Creamy Acorn Squash Soup 25
    Zucchini Soup with Rosemary 26
    Cream of Asparagus Soup 28
    Chicken & Broccoli Soup 29
    Mushroom Soup 30
    Tomato Soup 31
    Kale Soup with White Beans 32
    Turkey & Corn Soup 33
    Butternut Squash & Coconut Milk Soup 35
    Potato Soup 37

Chapter 5: Pureed Food 38
    Broccoli Puree 38
    Pureed Carrot 39
    Mashed Parsnips 40
    Vegetable Puree 41
    Carrot & Parsnip Puree 42
    Creamy Cauliflower Puree 43
    Pumpkin Puree 44
    Hummus 45
    Celery Root Puree 46
    Roasted Sweet Potato Puree 47

Chapter 6: Main Dishes 48

Greek Chicken 48
Tofu & Quinoa Bowl 49
Asian-Style Pork Tenderloin 51
Baked Chicken & Vegetables 52
Ginger Beef Stir Fry 53
Barbecue Salmon 55
Pork & Black Bean Stew 56
Fried Trout 57
Cajun Chicken 58
Creamy Chicken 59
Chicken Tikka Masala 60
Crispy Tuna Patties 62
Sweet & Sour Pork 63
Crispy Chicken 65
Chicken Casserole 66

Chapter 7: Snacks 67
Chicken & Cheese Steak Wrap 67
Pesto Pasta 68
Chicken Caprese 69
Turkey Turnover 70
Chicken Wrap 71
Chicken Rolls 73
Veggie Pizza 74
Stuffed Acorn Squash 75
Zucchini Boats 76
Stuffed French Toast 77

Chapter 8: Desserts 78
Pumpkin Mousse 78
Brownie Bites 79
Silky Fudge Dessert 80
Dessert Cups 81
Cheesecake Pudding 82
Jello 83
Cream Cheese Cookies 84
Spinach & Strawberry Salad 85
Chocolate Mousse 86
Chocolate Chip Cookies 87
Pudding Bites 88

Chapter 9: Salads 89
Green Salad 89
Summer Salad 91
Roasted Beet Salad 92
Carrot & Cucumber Salad 93
Cucumber Salad 94
Spinach & Cranberry Salad 95
Kale Salad 96
Mediterranean Salad 97
Broccoli Salad 98

Chapter 10: Drinks 99
Spinach & Banana Smoothie 99
Blackberry Lemonade 100
Green Smoothie 101
Watermelon Water 102
Blueberry Smoothie 103

Chapter 11: 4-Weekly Meal Plan 104
Conclusion 107

Introduction

A Low-Fodmap diet is designed to help people with irritable bowel syndrome (IBS) have better control over their symptoms by limiting certain foods. Fodmaps stands for fermentable oligo-saccharides, di-saccharides, mono-saccharides and polyols. Put more simply, Fodmaps are certain types of carbohydrates—the sugars, starches, and fiber in foods.

The Low-Fodmap diet is the long-awaited answer. In clinical trials, over three quarters of people with chronic digestive symptoms gain significant relief by reducing their intake of Fodmaps. The recipe is aimed to removing Fodmaps from your diet and banishing digestive pain forever. With easy guidelines and simple recipes, you'll learn how to identify and avoid Fodmap foods, and make healthy and delicious Fodmap free meals in your own kitchen.

Chapter 1: Overview of Low-Fodmap Diet

Key to a Healthy Gut

Our Gastrointestinal Gut (GI), bowel, or gut has a pivotal role to play in preserving the health and life of our systems. This is the first organic body system that notes rapid growth during the first 3 years of our lives and continues to develop for the rest of our lives. Its primary role is to digest and break down the food we consume and facilitate nutrient absorption or waste/elimination of unwanted substances whenever necessary. Gut was also surprisingly found to have connections with the brain (the gut-brain axis) and the immune system, indirectly affecting their health.

The human gut reportedly hosts over 100 trillion microorganisms, generally known as 'microbiota' or 'microflora'. These include both beneficial and health-preserving bacteria (probiotics) as well as bad bacteria and parasites that may lead to various health symptoms if their population spans out of control.

Essentially, there are two schools of thought when it comes to improving gut health. The first is to increase or feed the population of beneficial bacteria that resides on the gut and the second is the reduction of bad bacteria or elimination of triggering substances from foods that may aggravate gut health. In many cases, these two approaches are used in tandem for deeper and more long-lasting results. This is essentially the key to optimal gut health in the long run.

The low FODMAP diet works by eliminating certain food triggers and depriving the bacterial population of feeding nutrients that they need to survive. However, since the diet might starve bad as well as good bacteria during the elimination phase, it is always a good idea to supplement your diet with probiotics so you don't lose any beneficial bacteria along the process.

Low Fodmap Diet as a Lifestyle

As specified earlier, the low FODMAP diet is not another diet fab for losing weight and getting shredded. It's a lifestyle choice that will improve gut health temporarily or for longer periods, as long as it is followed wisely and in moderation. Since over 50 million Americans suffer from digestive problems on a chronic basis and the global prevalence according to multinational studies reaches 40% of the adult population, it would be wise to follow a diet and lifestyle that improves chronic gut health.

IBS especially is a common disturbance that affects over 25 million Americans and approx. 15% of the total population worldwide. Common symptoms include bloating, gas, and abdominal pain. The symptoms can range from mild to severe and in some cases, they are so extreme that they cause disability and failure to keep up with daily life tasks e.g., work. Hence, a diet that manages these symptoms e.g. the low FODMAP diet, is a diet that will give the sufferers their normal life back.

Many mistakenly think that the low FODMAP diet is only about the elimination of high FODMAP foods to control IBS symptoms but this isn't the case. The diet is only a part of a more holistic approach to achieving gut health. Paired with a healthy lifestyle e.g. no smoking, decreased stress, the effects of the diet will be more profound and lasting.

What Causes IBS and Digestive Disorders

Patients and doctors have noticed for quite a long time that certain foods and substances may trigger IBS and similar digestive symptoms e.g., gas, bloating irregular bowel movements. Some well-known food triggers, as mentioned earlier are lactose, fructose, alcohol, etc. These are often found in certain dairy products, legumes, nuts, grains, cruciferous veggies, and fruits. Some of these have been found to cause gas and should be avoided in cases of vivid bloating and indigestion. However, up until a few decades ago, these certain foods appeared in the lists of foods to avoid for IBS without exactly identifying the common chemical attributes that these food triggers shared. Eventually, with the progress of science and technology that took off the last 40 years, these chemical substances were identified and classified as potential triggers for people who experience IBS and other digestive problems. The poor digestion and malabsorption of these short chain carbs have been described by medical researchers as the culprit of gas, bloating, diarrhea, nausea, and abdominal pain in patients diagnosed with IBS. The earliest reports have identified 5 particular culprits, categorized based on their chemical form:

- Lactose. Early studies that date back to the 50s and 60s have found a link between lactose and diarrhea symptoms. Ever since there have been numerous lab diagnostic means to check lactose responses and diagnose intolerance. In intolerant patients with digestive issues, doctors have advised the elimination of lactose from the patient's diet, however, this has been found to ease only some symptoms of IBS and not solve the matter completely.
- Fructose & Sorbitol. Fructose is a type of monosaccharide sugar that is naturally found in fruits. Sorbitol is also similar to sugar alcohol and carb found in certain fruits like figs and plums. Although not many studies have found a clear link between fructose/sorbitol and IBS symptoms, a few studies have found that fructose or low fructose and sorbitol diet has eased IBS symptoms in patients that didn't respond to other methods of treatment or lactose elimination.
- Oligosaccharides. Oligosaccharides (oligos or oligo-fructans) stand for the "O" in "FODMAP" and refer to sugar alcohols that contain up to 10 linked monosaccharide units–in simple words, they are classified as "simple sugars". These include both natural and artificial sweeteners. Beans

and some veggies e.g. Jerusalem artichokes are also high in oligos. Our systems though have been found to lack the enzymes necessary to digest and fully absorb oligos, resulting in flatulence (gas) and constipation.
- Polyols. Polyols (standing for the "P" in FODMAP) are sugar alcohols that occur naturally in certain fruits and artificial sweeteners like mannitol and xylitol. Their ability to aggravate gut symptoms was first discovered in a 60s study and there have been studies ever since backing up the link between polyps and induced gut symptoms, especially when combined with fructose and sorbitol. However, in moderate doses polyps have been found to have a beneficial effect on the gut's biome, increasing the numbers of beneficial bacteria in the gut.

The common pattern here is that these substances lead collectively to indigestion (lactose), malabsorption (fructose, sorbitol, polyols), and fermentation (oligos) which ultimately lead to IBS and digestive disorders when they are consumed in high amounts.
Stress and other lifestyle factors may also be clear culprits of IBS symptoms; however, a few studies have found that they may worsen already existing symptoms in IBS-affected patients. Therefore, a low FODMAP diet followed periodically coupled with a healthy lifestyle may be the answer for the effective reduction of IBS symptoms.

Low Fodmap Diet Targets & Benefits

By now, you already realize that the main purpose of a low FODMAP diet is to treat IBS and other digestive problems. A short-term or occasionally followed low FODMAP diet has been found to effectively treat the symptoms that come with the fermentation, indigestion, or malabsorption of certain carbs and substances in those who are intolerant to these. More specifically, a low FODMAP diet can result in:

- Less gas/flatulence. Due to the decreased fermentation of sugar carbs in the digestive tract, the system will be able to release less gas. In one particular UK study, it has been found that 87% of the study participants who followed a low FODMAP diet have noted a significant decrease in gas production/flatulence as opposed to 49% of the control group.
- Less bloating. In the same study above, the study's subjects who followed a low FODMAP diet have shown an impressive decrease of their bloating symptoms by as much as 82% compared to 49% of those that did not follow the low FODMAP diet.
- Less abdominal pain. In a study involving big children aged 7-18, it has been found that the children who followed a low FODMAP diet had less intense abdominal pain episodes compared to the children participants who followed another diet type (TACD).
- Less diarrhea. A US study conducted in 110 adult patients with diarrhea-predominant IBS symptoms, has shown that the patients' group who followed a low FODMAP diet had fewer diarrhea episodes and noted better stool frequency than those who followed a GDA (Guideline Daily Amounts) diet.

Although symptoms and their severity may vary between IBS patients, there is plenty of evidence pointing out significant improvements in bloating, gas, abdominal pain, and diarrhea in patients who follow the diet for a few weeks. Therefore, if you experience any of the above, your symptoms will most likely improve, if you follow the low FODMAP diet properly.

List of Ingredients to Avoid

The actual foods and ingredients that are high on FODMAPS and may, in turn, aggravate IBS symptoms are the following (we have broken this down to 5 main categories and subcategories so you can check easily which foods to avoid when you are in the first stage of the low FODMAP diet).

Fruits:
- Apples
- Apricots
- Blackberries
- Cherries
- Mangoes
- Nectarines
- Pears
- Plums
- Prunes
- Watermelon
- Dried fruits e.g. apricots, figs, etc.

Vegetables:
- Artichokes
- Asparagus
- Beetroot
- Broccoli
- Brussel sprouts
- Cauliflower
- Celery
- Garlic
- Leeks
- Mushrooms
- Onions
- Sweet Corn

Legumes:
- Beans (all kinds)
- Lentils

Nuts:
- Cashew Nuts
- Pistachios

Sugars:
- Agave nectar
- Corn Syrup
- Fructose
- Honey
- Maltitol
- Sorbitol
- Xylitol

Wheat products (with gluten):
- Cereals
- Crackers

- Bread
- Pasta
- Pizza

Dairy:
- Cow milk
- Custard
- Ice cream
- Pudding
- Soft cheeses e.g. cottage cheese
- Yogurt

Drinks:
- Alcohol
- Sports & energy drinks with artificial sweeteners

Best Tips to Succeed In the Kitchen With Low Fodmap Diet

Following a low FODMAP diet can be a tad challenging for newbies, however, don't let the list of "foods to avoid" fool you and limit your cooking options. There are just as many if not more cooking ingredients to explore and you can prepare low FODMAP meals much easier if you follow these kitchen tips. Here they are:

Tip #1: Prepare your meals in advance.

If you don't have the time and energy to prepare your low FODMAP meal for the day, choose 1-2 days a week based on your schedule to prepare a week's worth of low FODMAP meals in advance. Make a shopping list of what you'll need (in case you don't have the necessary recipe ingredients already), go shopping, and spare 2-3 hours every time to prepare your weekly meals. You can also keep any leftovers in the freezer if you plan to prepare larger batches of food.

Tip#2: Make your condiments and dressings.

Most store-bought condiments and dressings e.g ketchup contain hidden amounts of processed or natural sugars which are the worst triggering FODMAPs for IBS patients. If you are not sure whether a condiment or dressing is low FODMAP, check its label and avoid anything that contains corn syrup, maltitol, fructose, or any other sugar from the prohibited list. If the recipe calls it, prepare your own using natural ingredients and low FODMAP sweetener alternatives such as maple syrup or Stevia.

Tip# 3: Go for lactose-free dairy options.

There is no need to quit eating dairy altogether when you are on a low FODMAP diet as there are some dairy options that contain low to zero amounts of lactose and thus are low on FODMAPs. Some good low or lactose-free options include dry/mature cheeses, lactose-free milk, and lactose-free yogurt. Vegetarian dairy alternatives like almond milk and soy yogurt are perfectly fine as long as they don't contain any FODMAP sugar types.

Tip#4: Use spices in place of onions and garlic.

Avoiding onions and garlic is a bit challenging as most recipes nowadays use these to add some flavor and dimension to the dish, however, you can counteract their lack by using flavorful spices e.g. curry, coriander, cumin, chili flakes. Nearly all spices (apart from garlic and onion powder obviously) are perfectly fine to use in a low FODMAP diet and there is no limit to their amounts--it's a matter of how hot or spicy you like your food.

Tip#5: Saute your meat and veggies first.

In addition to using spices in your dishes in place of onion and garlic, you can add more flavor to your dishes by browning your meat and veggies first in a bit of vegetable oil. You can also make your onion and garlic-free stock by browning low FODMAP veggies e.g carrots and parsnips and adding at least 4 cups of boiling water, salt, herbs, and spices. Once your stock is ready, you can keep it in the fridge for up to 1 week (to use later on your weekly meals) or in the freezer for up to 2 months, in the form of ice-cubes so you can use 1-2 cubes every time you need it for the recipe.

Positive Vibes from the Author

Following a low FODMAP diet isn't as challenging as some people assume. If you prepare your meals in advance, check your portions, and experiment with low FODMAP alternatives for at least a week, things will be much easier afterward. Keep in mind that during the final stages, you may re-introduce some foods that are higher in FODMAPs to see your gut's reaction, and based on our research, most people are affected by one type of FODMAP more than others. So don't worry, you won't have to quit eating all the foods on the prohibited list for long periods and restrict yourself. And if you are stuck or don't know what else you should cook, check out our recipes or join an online FODMAP diet community to draw some inspiration and support from people like you who are already following the diet. Even better, you may seek the professional advice and support of a nutritionist who has experience in treating patients with digestive disorders, especially IBS. Don't be afraid to ask for help sometimes it's best to have someone on your side instead of going through your diet journey alone.

Remember: Low FODMAP is not just another diet fad, it's a lifestyle choice and your gut will thank you for it!

Chapter 2: Overview of Meal Prep

What is Meal Prepping?

Meal prepping is planning and cooking food ahead of time, usually a few days to an entire week. There are multiple methods to meal prepping that would suit your lifestyle or preference.

You can assemble raw ingredients of recipes and freeze them, batch cook different food to reduce cooking times, or cook entire meals and store them in individual containers.

Benefits of Meal Prepping

- Saves you lots of time. You can save up to 10 hours per week from cooking and food preparation.
- You don't have to rely on willpower when deciding what to eat because it is already made for you.
- Meal prepping makes it easier to follow a healthy diet plan and eliminates the temptation of unhealthy eating and going beyond your planned portion size.
- Tracking your calorie intake will be a lot easier.
- Buying food in bulk will save you a lot of money.

Tips for Success

Meal prepping has a lot of benefits, especially for those with very strict dietary requirements such as a bariatric diet. Here are some useful tips to help you reach your dietary goals while on recovery from bariatric surgery.

1. **Create a meal plan**

Different people have different dietary needs, that is why we need to plan our meals according to our nutritional goals. Your dietician, health practitioner, or nutritionist can help you determine what foods to eat and how much. Look for recipes or cookbooks suited for the bariatric diet to guide you with meal planning. There are also websites and mobile apps where you can check to know how many calories you'll be getting to make sure you don't exceed the daily recommended consumption.

2. **Formulate a routine**

One of the biggest advantages of meal prepping is that it is a time saver. Building a weekly schedule will make meal prepping easier and less of a chore. Choose a day in a week when you will go grocery shopping and cooking your meals.

3. **Always buy in bulk**

Choose those that do not spoil easily or can be stored in the freezer. Organic quinoa, light brown rice, olive oil, and frozen vegetables can be purchased in bulk to last you a few months. Buying produce that is in season will also help you save money.

4. **Invest in good quality cooking utensils and appliances**

There are several multi-cookers available in the market today to make cooking a breeze and further cut cooking times. Big pots and pans are excellent for cooking large batches of food at a time. A food processor or vegetable slicer will also come in handy for meal preps.

5. **Choose a meal prep style that suits you**

You can prep entire meals that only need re-heating, or you can batch cook several ingredients separately to cut down on cooking times.

6. **Get plenty storage**

Opt for glass containers for your pre-prepared meals. You may also go for air-tight plastic containers, just make sure that it is BPA-free if you plan on microwaving your meals in them. Stainless steel food containers are also excellent choices.

Glass mason jars also come in handy for storing wet and dry ingredients like grains and dressings. Try silicone baggies and beeswax wraps to lessen your plastic use, they are perfect for snacking on-the-go. Also, get stackable versions of these containers to save space on your fridge.

7. **Label your foods**

With so many containers in your fridge, it's easy to forget some and end up with spoiled food. To make it easier to keep track and mainly for safety, make it a habit of marking or using labels to make sure you consume them promptly. You may also use your phone calendar to list your daily meals and set a reminder. Knowing about food safety measures is an important thing to consider when you are meal prepping while on a bariatric diet. Read it to guide you with the right cooking temperatures for different foods and learn about other best practices.

8. Don't mix the sauce or dressing with the dry ingredients

Pouring sauces over your cooked chicken or rice will make it soggy. Unless you are aiming for this kind of texture, store wet ingredients in mason jars.

9. Prepare snacks too

You don't have to stick to meals. Pre-packing snacks for whenever you get hungry in between meals are equally important as it keeps you from eating anything that might upset your stomach or mess with your goals.

10. Try shopping online

Look for businesses that offer this option around your area. You may also ask your local supermarket if they have this option available. Not only is this convenient, but you'll further cut down on costs if you do your shopping online. Also, it is much less tempting to go beyond your grocery list and budget versus being physically at the store.

Chapter 3: Breakfast

Breakfast Popsicle

Preparation Time: 5 hours and 5 minutes
Cooking Time: 0 minute
Servings: 6

Ingredients:

- 1 cup plain Greek yogurt (non-fat)
- ½ cup almond milk
- ½ cup oats
- 1 cup mixed berries

Method:

1. Combine all ingredients.
2. Pour mixture into popsicle molds.
3. Freeze for 5 hours.
4. Serve when ready to eat.

Nutritional Content:

- Calories: 75
- Fat: 0.6 g
- Cholesterol: 3 mg
- Sodium: 36 mg
- Carbohydrates: 11 g
- Dietary Fiber: 1.5 g
- Sugar: 4 g
- Protein: 5 g

Cottage Cheese Pancake

Preparation Time: 5 minutes
Cooking Time: 5 minutes
Servings: 4

Ingredients:

- ½ tsp baking soda
- ⅓ cup all-purpose flour
- 1 cup low-fat cottage cheese
- 3 eggs, beaten
- ½ tablespoon oil

Method:

1. Mix all ingredients except oil in a bowl.
2. Add oil to the pan over medium heat.
3. Store batter in a food container.
4. Refrigerate until ready to cook.
5. When ready to cook, pour batter into the pan.
6. Flip once bubbles appear.
7. Cook for 2 to 3 minutes or until firm.

Nutritional Content:

- Calories: 152
- Fat: 7 g
- Cholesterol: 2 mg
- Carbohydrate: 10 g
- Sodium: 385 mg
- Sugar: 2 g
- Protein: 13 g

Pumpkin Oatmeal

Preparation Time: 5 minutes
Cooking Time: 3 minutes
Servings: 1

Ingredients:

- ¼ cup rolled oats
- ⅛ teaspoon cinnamon
- ½ cup pumpkin puree
- Pinch ground ginger
- Pinch ground cloves
- ½ cup salt-free cottage cheese
- 1 teaspoon Truvia baking blend

Method:

1. Add all ingredients except cheese to a microwave-safe dish or bowl.
2. Mix well.
3. Microwave on high setting for 80 to 90 seconds.
4. Add cottage cheese. Microwave on high for 1 minute
5. Store in a glass jar with lid and refrigerate for up to 1 day.

Nutritional Content:

- Calories: 205
- Fat: 3 g
- Cholesterol: 3 mg
- Sodium: 312 mg
- Carbohydrates: 34 g
- Dietary Fiber: 7 g
- Sugar: 9 g
- Protein: 14 g

Broccoli & Tofu Scramble

Preparation Time: 10 minutes
Cooking Time: 10 minutes
Servings: 6

Ingredients:

- 1 tablespoon oil
- 1 onion, chopped
- ¼ lb. mushrooms, chopped
- ½ lb. broccoli, chopped
- 1½ lb. tofu, sliced into cubes
- 3 eggs, beaten

Method:

1. Preheat your oven to 350 degrees F.
2. Add oil to a pan over medium heat.
3. Cook onion and mushrooms for 1 minute.
4. Push to one side.
5. Add tofu and broccoli.
6. Cook until tofu cubes are golden.
7. Add mixture to a bowl with the eggs.
8. Put the egg mixture back to the pan.
9. Cook until eggs are set.
10. Store in food container and refrigerate.

Nutritional Content:

- Calories: 190
- Fat: 8g
- Cholesterol: 0 mg
- Sodium: 350 mg
- Carbohydrates: 18g
- Dietary fiber: 4g
- Sugar: 3g
- Protein: 13g

Baked Spinach & Cottage Cheese

Preparation Time: 10 minutes
Cooking Time: 30 minutes
Servings: 8

Ingredients:

- 2 cups non-fat cottage cheese
- 2 eggs, beaten
- 10 oz. spinach

Method:

1. Preheat oven to 350 degrees F.
2. Combine cheese, eggs and spinach in a bowl.
3. Pour into a baking pan.
4. Bake for 30 minutes.
5. Store in food container and refrigerate.

Nutritional Content:

- Calories: 78
- Fat: 3 g
- Cholesterol: 0 mg
- Carbohydrates: 3 g
- Fiber: 1 g
- Sugars: 2 g
- Protein: 11 g

Baked Eggs with Broccoli

Preparation Time: 15 minutes
Cooking Time: 1 hour and 30 minutes
Servings: 8

Ingredients:

- 1 teaspoon olive oil
- 6 eggs, beaten
- ½ cup mushrooms, sliced
- 10 oz. broccoli florets, chopped
- Pinch paprika
- Salt and pepper to taste

Method:

1. Preheat your oven to 350 degrees F.
2. Mix all ingredients in a bowl.
3. Add mixture to a baking pan.
4. Bake in the oven for 1 hour and 30 minutes.
5. Store in food container and refrigerate.
6. Reheat before serving.

Nutritional Content:

- Calories: 115
- Fat: 5 g
- Cholesterol: 75 mg
- Carbohydrate: 5 g
- Sodium: 419 mg
- Sugar: 2 g
- Protein: 12 g

Breakfast Strawberry Wrap

Preparation Time: 5 minutes
Cooking Time: 0 minute
Servings: 1

Ingredients:

- 1 whole wheat tortilla
- 1 tablespoon low-sugar strawberry jam
- 3 tablespoons ricotta cheese
- ¼ cup strawberries, sliced

Method:

1. Spread the tortilla with strawberry jam and ricotta cheese.
2. Top with the strawberry slices.
3. Roll up.
4. Store in food container and refrigerate.

Nutritional Content:

- Calories: 233
- Fat: 9 g
- Cholesterol: 24 mg
- Carbohydrate: 30 g
- Sodium: 229 mg
- Sugar: 8 g
- Protein: 8 g

Breakfast Enchilada

Preparation Time: 5 minutes
Cooking Time: 3 minutes
Servings: 1

Ingredients:

- 1 egg white, beaten
- 1 egg, beaten
- Cooking spray
- Salt and pepper to taste
- 1 oz. tofu, sliced into cubes and cooked
- 2 tablespoons salsa
- 1 tablespoon low-fat Mexican cheese, shredded

Method:

1. Mix egg white and egg in a bowl.
2. Spray a pan with oil.
3. Place the pan over medium heat.
4. Add the eggs and cook for 1 to 2 minutes without stirring.
5. Season with salt and pepper.
6. Flip and cook for another 1 minute.
7. Transfer to a plate.
8. Cook eggs on the other side about two minutes or until completely cooked and transfer to a plate.
9. Top the egg with tofu and cheese.
10. Roll it up.
11. Store in a food container.
12. Refrigerate for up to 1 day.
13. Reheat when ready to serve.
14. Serve with salsa.

Nutritional Content:

- Calories: 171
- Fat: 8 g
- Cholesterol: 0 mg
- Carbohydrate: 3 g
- Protein: 23 g
- Sodium: 432 mg
- Sugar: 3 g

Breakfast Sandwich

Preparation Time: 5 minutes
Cooking Time: 0 minute
Servings: 3

Ingredients:

- 1 apple, chopped
- 6 oz. canned tuna flakes in water, drained
- 1 teaspoon mustard
- ¼ cup low-fat vanilla yogurt
- 6 slices whole wheat bread
- 3 lettuces leaves

Method:

1. Mix apple, tuna flakes, mustard and yogurt in a bowl.
2. Spread mixture on top of the 3 bread slices.
3. Add lettuce and top with the other bread slice.
4. Store in food container.
5. Refrigerate for up to 1 day.

Nutritional Content:

- Calories: 250
- Fat: 2.5 g
- Cholesterol: 28 mg
- Sodium: 330 mg
- Carbohydrates: 30 g
- Sugar: 5.25 g
- Dietary Fiber: 5 g
- Protein: 23 g

Egg Muffin

Preparation Time: 10 minutes
Cooking Time: 20 minutes
Servings: 12

Ingredients:

- Cooking spray
- 12 turkey bacon slices, cooked and sliced
- 6 eggs, beaten
- ½ cup almond milk
- ¾ cup low-fat Swiss cheese
- ¼ teaspoon Italian seasoning
- Salt and pepper to taste

Method:

1. Spray muffin pan with oil.
2. Preheat your oven to 350 degrees F.
3. Add bacon to the muffin cups.
4. In a bowl, mix the remaining ingredients.
5. Pour mixture into the muffin cups.
6. Bake in the oven for 20 minutes.
7. Transfer egg muffins to food container.
8. Refrigerate for up to 1 day.
9. Reheat before serving.

Nutritional Content:

- Calories: 98
- Fat: 7g
- Cholesterol: 7 mg
- Carbohydrates: 1g
- Fiber: 0g
- Sugar: 1g
- Protein: 8g

Chapter 4: Soup

Creamy Acorn Squash Soup

Preparation Time: 10 minutes
Cooking Time: 40 minutes
Servings: 6

Ingredients:

- 2 tablespoons coconut oil
- 2 onions, sliced
- 3 acorn squash, sliced in half and roasted
- 1 ½ cups vegetable broth
- ¾ cup coconut milk
- 1 tablespoon curry powder

Method:

1. Add coconut oil to a soup pot over medium heat.
2. Cook onion for 1 to 2 minutes.
3. Stir in the squash.
4. Pour in the broth and coconut milk.
5. Add the curry powder.
6. Mix well.
7. Bring to a boil.
8. Simmer for 30 minutes.
9. Turn off heat and let cool.
10. Transfer to a food processor.
11. Process to puree.
12. Store in food containers and freeze for up to 1 month.
13. Reheat when ready to serve.

Nutritional Content:

- Calories: 283
- Fat: 18 g
- Cholesterol: 1 mg
- Sodium: 120 mg
- Carbohydrates: 29 g
- Fiber: 4 g
- Sugar: 2 g
- Protein: 4 g

Zucchini Soup with Rosemary

Preparation Time: 30 minutes
Cooking Time: 40 minutes
Servings: 8

Ingredients:

- 1 tablespoon vegetable oil
- 2 tablespoons butter
- 1 onion, chopped
- 2 teaspoons fresh rosemary, minced
- 2 cloves garlic, sliced
- 1 potato, sliced
- 4 cups vegetable broth
- 3 zucchinis, sliced
- Green onions, chopped

Method:

1. Add oil and butter to a pan over medium high heat.
2. Cook onion for 5 minutes.
3. Stir in rosemary and garlic.
4. Cook for 2 minutes.
5. Add potato and broth.
6. Bring to a boil and simmer for 10 minutes.
7. Stir in zucchini and simmer for 15 minutes.
8. Turn off heat.
9. Let cool.
10. Transfer to a food processor.
11. Process until pureed.
12. Reheat.
13. Top with green onions.
14. Transfer to food container.
15. Freeze for up to 1 month.
16. Reheat before serving.

Nutritional Content:

- Calories: 89
- Fat: 2 g
- Cholesterol: 8 mg
- Sodium: 12 mg
- Carbohydrates: 10 g
- Fiber: 2 g
- Sugar: 2.5 g
- Protein: 3 g

Cream of Asparagus Soup

Preparation Time: 10 minutes
Cooking Time: 20 minutes
Servings: 4

Ingredients:

- 1 tablespoon olive oil
- 1 clove garlic, minced
- 1 onion, sliced
- 1 carrot, chopped
- 1 stalk celery, chopped
- 10 ½ oz. asparagus, chopped
- 2 cups vegetable stock
- 1 cup water
- 1 cup almond milk
- Salt and pepper to taste

Method:

1. Add oil to a pan over medium heat.
2. Cook garlic, onion, carrot and celery for 10 minutes, stirring often.
3. Add asparagus, stock, water and almond milk.
4. Season with salt and pepper.
5. Bring to a boil.
6. Simmer for 10 minutes.
7. Let cool.
8. Transfer to food processor.
9. Pulse until smooth.
10. Freeze for up to 1 month.

Nutritional Content:

- Calories: 203
- Fat: 5 g
- Cholesterol: 0 mg
- Sodium: 262 mg
- Carbohydrates: 29 g
- Fiber: 8 g
- Sugar: 4 g
- Protein: 10 g

Chicken & Broccoli Soup

Preparation Time: 20 minutes
Cooking Time: 40 minutes
Servings: 6

Ingredients:

- Cooking spray
- ½ cup onion, chopped
- ½ cup celery, chopped
- 1 cup broccoli florets, chopped
- ½ cup carrot, chopped
- 4 cups reduced-sodium chicken stock
- ½ teaspoon dried basil
- ½ teaspoon dried oregano
- ½ teaspoon dried thyme
- 1 lb. chicken breasts, cooked and shredded
- 12 oz. milk
- 1 tablespoon Worcestershire sauce

Method:

1. Spray your pot with oil.
2. Place pot over medium heat.
3. Add onion, celery, broccoli and carrot to the pot.
4. Cook for 5 minutes.
5. Add stock and dried herbs.
6. Simmer for 15 to 20 minutes.
7. Add milk, chicken and Worcestershire sauce.
8. Cook for 5 minutes.

Nutritional Content:

- Calories: 260
- Fat: 2.5 g
- Cholesterol: 20 mg
- Sodium: 12 mg
- Carbohydrates: 25 g
- Fiber: 6 g
- Sugar: 8.5 g
- Protein: 31 g

Mushroom Soup

Preparation Time: 10 minutes
Cooking Time: 25 minutes
Servings: 2

Ingredients:

- 1 tablespoon coconut oil
- 1 onion, chopped
- 2 cloves garlic, chopped
- 10 ½ oz. mushrooms, sliced
- 1 stalk celery, sliced
- 1 cup vegetable stock
- 1 cup oat milk
- Salt and pepper to taste

Method:

1. Pour oil into a pot over medium heat.
2. Cook onion, garlic, mushrooms and celery for 10 minutes.
3. Stir in the remaining ingredients.
4. Bring to a boil.
5. Simmer for 15 minutes.
6. Turn off heat.
7. Let cool.
8. Transfer to food container.
9. Process until pureed.
10. Store in food container.
11. Freeze for up to 1 month.
12. Reheat before serving.

Nutritional Content:

- Calories: 385
- Fat: 10 g
- Cholesterol: 0 mg
- Sodium: 526 mg
- Carbohydrates: 57 g
- Fiber: 3 g
- Sugar: 6 g
- Protein: 21 g

Tomato Soup

Preparation Time: 10 minutes
Cooking Time: 30 minutes
Servings: 4

Ingredients:

- 1 teaspoon olive oil
- 1 teaspoon garlic, minced
- 14 oz. tomatoes, chopped
- 28 oz. canned tomatoes
- 1 teaspoon Italian seasoning
- ¼ cup Parmesan cheese
- Salt and pepper to taste

Method:

1. Add oil to a pot over medium heat.
2. Add garlic and cook for 30 seconds, stirring often.
3. Add the rest of the ingredients.
4. Simmer for 20 to 25 minutes.
5. Turn off heat.
6. Let cool.
7. Transfer to a food processor.
8. Blend until smooth.
9. Transfer to food container.
10. Freeze until ready to serve.
11. Reheat before serving.

Nutritional Content:

- Calories: 157
- Fat: 3.2
- Cholesterol: 2 mg
- Sodium: 10 mg
- Carbohydrates: 3.2 g
- Fiber: 3 g
- Sugar: 5 g
- Protein: 24 g

Kale Soup with White Beans

Preparation Time: 10 minutes
Cooking Time: 30 minutes
Servings: 4

Ingredients:

- 1 tablespoon avocado oil
- 1 onion, chopped
- 3 stalks celery, chopped
- 3 potatoes, diced
- 3 carrots, chopped
- Salt and pepper to taste
- 4 cloves garlic, minced
- 2 tablespoons Italian seasoning
- 30 oz. white beans, rinsed and drained
- 32 oz. vegetable broth
- 26 oz. canned diced tomatoes
- 1 cup kale, chopped

Method:

1. Pour oil into a pot over medium heat.
2. Cook the onion, celery, carrots and potatoes for 7 to 8 minutes.
3. Season with salt.
4. Add garlic and Italian seasoning.
5. Cook for 1 minute.
6. Add the rest of the ingredients except kale.
7. Bring to a boil.
8. Simmer for 20 minutes.
9. Add kale and cook for 1 minute.
10. Let cool.
11. Store in food containers and freeze for up to 1 month.

Nutritional Content:

- Calories: 309
- Fat: 3 g
- Cholesterol: 0 mg
- Sodium: 126 mg
- Carbohydrates: 57 g
- Fiber: 12 g
- Sugar: 12 g
- Protein: 15 g

Turkey & Corn Soup

Preparation Time: 20 minutes
Cooking Time: 30 minutes
Servings: 6

Ingredients:

- 1 teaspoon olive oil
- 1 onion, diced
- 2 cloves garlic, minced
- 1 red bell pepper, chopped
- 1 stalk celery, diced
- 4 oz. canned diced green chili
- 3 cups reduced-sodium chicken broth
- 1 ¼ cups corn kernels
- 2 cups almond milk
- ¼ cup all-purpose flour
- 2 cups turkey, cooked and shredded
- Green onion, chopped

Method:

1. Add olive oil to a pan over medium heat.
2. Cook onion, garlic, bell pepper and celery for 5 minutes.
3. Stir in green chili.
4. Cook for 1 minute.
5. Add chicken broth.
6. Bring to a boil.
7. Reduce heat and simmer for 10 minutes.
8. Stir in corn and simmer for 5 minutes.
9. Mix milk and flour in a bowl.
10. Add mixture to the soup.
11. Cook for 15 minutes.
12. Add turkey and green onions.
13. Let cool.
14. Transfer to food container.
15. Freeze for up to 1 month.

16. Reheat before serving.

Nutritional Content:

- Calories: 223.3
- Fat: 6.6 g
- Cholesterol: 13 mg
- Sodium: 143 mg
- Carbohydrates: 25 g
- Fiber: 1.6 g
- Sugar: 8.8 g
- Protein: 15.6 g

Butternut Squash & Coconut Milk Soup

Preparation Time: 15 minutes
Cooking Time: 45 minutes
Servings: 6

Ingredients:

- 2 tablespoons olive oil
- 1 white onion, chopped
- 1 ¼ tsp. ginger, crushed
- 3 cloves garlic, crushed
- 1 butternut squash, sliced and roasted
- Salt to taste
- ¼ tsp. cinnamon powder
- 15 oz. coconut milk
- 2 cups vegetable broth

Method:

1. Add olive oil to a pot over medium heat.
2. Cook onion, ginger and garlic for 3 minutes.
3. Stir in butternut squash slices
4. Season with salt and cinnamon powder.
5. Cook for 3 minutes.
6. Pour in milk and broth.
7. Bring to a boil.
8. Simmer for 30 minutes.
9. Turn off heat.
10. Let cool.
11. Transfer to food processor.
12. Pulse until smooth.
13. Transfer to food container.
14. Freeze for up to 1 month.
15. Reheat before serving.

Nutritional Content:

- Calories: 321
- Fat: 3 g

- Cholesterol: 0 mg
- Sodium: 415 mg
- Carbohydrates: 32 g
- Fiber: 5 g
- Sugar: 6 g
- Protein: 4 g

Potato Soup

Preparation Time: 10 minutes
Cooking Time: 1 hour
Servings: 4

Ingredients:

- Water
- 4 cups potatoes, chopped
- 4 cups vegetable broth
- 1 tablespoon olive oil
- 1 onion, chopped
- Salt and pepper to taste
- Green onions, chopped

Method:

1. Fill a pot with water.
2. Boil potatoes for 20 to 30 minutes.
3. Drain the water.
4. In a pan over medium heat, add the oil and onion.
5. Cook for 3 minutes.
6. Put the potatoes back to the pan along with the broth.
7. Season with salt and pepper.
8. Cover the pot.
9. Cook for 30 minutes.
10. Turn off heat.
11. Let cool.
12. Transfer mixture to a food processor.
13. Puree and store in food containers.
14. Freeze for up to 1 month.
15. Reheat before serving.

Nutritional Content:

- Calories: 12
- Fat: 5 g
- Cholesterol: 0 mg
- Sodium: 21 mg
- Carbohydrates: 24 g
- Fiber: 3 g
- Sugar: 0 g
- Protein: 8 g

Chapter 5: Pureed Food

Broccoli Puree

Preparation Time: 10 minutes
Cooking Time: 30 minutes
Servings: 4

Ingredients:

- Water
- 4 cups broccoli florets
- 2 tablespoons vegan butter
- ½ cup heavy cream
- Pinch ground nutmeg

Method:

1. Fill a pot with water.
2. Place it over medium heat.
3. Boil the broccoli for 20 minutes.
4. Drain and rinse.
5. Add to the broccoli to a food processor along with the rest of the ingredients. Pulse until smooth.
6. Store in food container.
7. Refrigerate for up to 3 days.

Nutritional Content:

- Calories: 200
- Fat: 17.4 g
- Cholesterol: 12 mg
- Sodium: 102 mg
- Carbohydrates: 9.9 g
- Fiber: 3.6 g
- Sugar: 2 g
- Protein: 4.5 g

Pureed Carrot

Preparation Time: 10 minutes
Cooking Time: 30 minutes
Servings: 4

Ingredients:

- 2 lb. carrots, sliced
- Water
- Salt and pepper to taste

Method:

1. Add carrots to a pan over medium heat.
2. Fill pan with water.
3. Bring to a boil.
4. Reduce heat.
5. Simmer for 20 minutes.
6. Drain.
7. Transfer carrots to a blender.
8. Puree until smooth.
9. Season with salt and pepper.

Nutritional Content:

- Calories: 120
- Fat: 4 g
- Cholesterol: 2 mg
- Carbohydrate: 10 g
- Sodium: 200 mg
- Sugar: 2 g
- Protein: 6 g

Mashed Parsnips

Preparation Time: 10 minutes
Cooking Time: 30 minutes
Servings: 8

Ingredients:

- 5 cups nut milk
- 10 parsnips, sliced into cubes
- Salt and pepper to taste
- 1 teaspoon dried thyme

Method:

1. Add milk to a pot over medium heat.
2. Heat for 1 minute.
3. Add parsnips and simmer for 30 minutes.
4. Mash parsnips on a plate.
5. Stir in 1 cup of the warm milk along with the salt, pepper and thyme.
6. Store in food container.
7. Serve within the day.

Nutritional Content:

- Calories: 143.2
- Fat: 10.7 g
- Cholesterol: 30.5 mg
- Sodium: 392.7 mg
- Carbohydrates: 7.1 g
- Fiber: 0.1 g
- Sugar: 6.9 g
- Protein: 5 g

Vegetable Puree

Preparation Time: 15 minutes
Cooking Time: 45 minutes
Servings: 8

Ingredients:

- 30 oz. vegetable broth
- 6 oz. mushrooms, sliced
- 1 carrot, sliced
- 1 potato, sliced into cubes
- ½ cup corn kernels
- 1 turnip, sliced into cubes
- ¼ cup cabbage, shredded
- ½ cup green peas
- Pinch Italian seasoning

Method:

1. Boil all the vegetables in the broth for 40 minutes.
2. Drain.
3. Add to a food processor.
4. Pulse until pureed.
5. Sprinkle with Italian seasoning.
6. Transfer to a food container.
7. Refrigerate for up to 3 days.

Nutritional Content:

- Calories: 66.7
- Fat: 0.5
- Cholesterol: 0 mg
- Sodium: 102 mg
- Carbohydrates: 14.1 g
- Fiber: 2.6 g
- Sugar: 4.6 g
- Protein: 2.3 g

Carrot & Parsnip Puree

Preparation Time: 15 minutes
Cooking Time: 20 minutes
Servings: 4

Ingredients:

- 2 carrots, sliced
- 8 parsnips, sliced into cubes
- Water
- ¼ cup chives, snipped
- 6 tablespoons vegan butter
- Pepper to taste

Method:

1. Add carrots and parsnips to a pot.
2. Cover with water.
3. Boil for 20 minutes. Drain.
4. Mash the vegetables using a potato masher.
5. Stir in remaining ingredients.
6. Transfer to a food container.
7. Refrigerate for up to 3 days.

Nutritional Content:

- Calories: 164.3
- Fat: 0.5 g
- Cholesterol: 45.8 mg
- Sodium: 220.5 mg
- Carbohydrates: 2.7 g
- Fiber: 3 g
- Sugar: 2 g
- Protein: 0.5 g

Creamy Cauliflower Puree

Preparation Time: 5 minutes
Cooking Time: 0 minute
Servings: 4

Ingredients:

- 4 teaspoons olive oil
- 3 cloves garlic, cooked
- 4 cups cauliflower florets, steamed
- ¼ cup nonfat milk
- ½ teaspoon black pepper
- ½ teaspoon garlic salt

Method:

1. Combine all ingredients to a food processor.
2. Pulse until smooth.
3. Store in an airtight container.
4. Refrigerate for up to 3 days.

Nutritional Content:

- Calories: 113
- Fat: 6 g
- Protein: 5 g
- Carbohydrate: 13 g
- Cholesterol: 3 mg
- Sodium: 383 mg
- Sugar: 6 g

Pumpkin Puree

Preparation Time: 10 minutes
Cooking Time: 1 hour
Servings: 4

Ingredients:

- 1 pumpkin, sliced in half, seeds removed

Method:

1. Preheat your oven to 325 degrees F.
2. Cover the pumpkin with foil.
3. Bake in the oven for 1 hour.
4. Let cool.
5. Scrape the flesh.
6. Add to a food processor.
7. Pulse until smooth.
8. Transfer to food container.
9. Refrigerate for up to 3 days or freeze for up to 1 month.

Nutritional Content:

- Calories: 188
- Fat: 0.7 g
- Cholesterol: 0 mg
- Sodium: 7 mg
- Carbohydrates: 47.2 g
- Fiber: 3.6 g
- Sugar: 9.9 g
- Protein: 7.3 g

Hummus

Preparation Time: 10 minutes
Cooking Time: 0 minute
Servings: 12

Ingredients:

- 15 oz. chickpeas, rinsed and drained
- 1 clove garlic, crushed
- 3 tablespoons olive oil
- 3 tablespoons lemon juice
- ½ teaspoon salt
- 1 tablespoon tahini

Method:

1. Add all ingredients to a food processor.
2. Process until smooth.
3. Store in an airtight container.
4. Refrigerate for up to 1 week.

Nutritional Content:

- Calories: 72
- Fat: 4.5 g
- Protein: 1.5 g
- Carbohydrate: 7.5 g
- Cholesterol: 0 mg
- Sodium: 149 mg
- Sugar: 0 g

Celery Root Puree

Preparation Time: 15 minutes
Cooking Time: 15 minutes
Servings: 6

Ingredients:

- 2 tablespoons lemon juice, divided
- 1 celery root, sliced
- Water
- ¼ cup heavy whipping cream
- Pinch cayenne pepper

Method:

1. Add 1 tablespoon lemon juice and celery root to a pot of water.
2. Bring to a boil.
3. Reduce heat.
4. Simmer for 20 minutes.
5. Drain and let cool.
6. Add the mixture to your food processor.
7. Stir in the cream, cayenne pepper and remaining lemon juice.
8. Process until pureed.
9. Store in food container.
10. Refrigerate for up to 3 days.

Nutritional Content:

- Calories: 139.4
- Fat: 2.5 g
- Cholesterol: 28 mg
- Sodium: 232.9 mg
- Carbohydrates: 14.7 g
- Fiber: 3.3 g
- Sugar: 2.2 g
- Protein: 9 g

Roasted Sweet Potato Puree

Preparation Time: 10 minutes
Cooking Time: 1 hour
Servings: 6

Ingredients:

- Olive oil
- 3 lb. sweet potatoes, sliced
- Pepper to taste

Method:

1. Add sweet potatoes to a baking pan.
2. Drizzle with olive oil.
3. Bake in the oven for 1 hour.
4. Let cool.
5. Transfer to a food processor.
6. Pulse until smooth.
7. Store in food container.
8. Refrigerate for up to 3 days.

Nutritional Content:

- Calories: 238.1
- Fat: 9.4
- Cholesterol: 25 mg
- Sodium: 322 mg
- Carbohydrates: 35.7 g
- Fiber: 5.1 g
- Sugar: 8.5 g
- Protein: 3.8 g

Chapter 6: Main Dishes

Greek Chicken

Preparation Time: 15 minutes
Cooking Time: 45 minutes
Servings: 4

Ingredients:

- 1 teaspoon garlic powder
- ½ cup Parmesan cheese, grated
- 1 cup plain Greek yogurt
- Salt and pepper to taste
- Cooking spray
- 4 chicken breast fillets

Method:

1. Preheat your oven to 375 degrees.
2. In a bowl, mix the garlic powder, Parmesan cheese, yogurt, salt and pepper.
3. Cover your baking pan with foil.
4. Spray it with foil.
5. Spread yogurt mixture on both sides of chicken.
6. Add to the baking pan.
7. Bake for 45 minutes.
8. Let cool.
9. Transfer to food containers.
10. Refrigerate for up to 2 days.
11. Serve with steamed vegetables.

Nutritional Content:

- Calories: 266
- Fat: 4g
- Cholesterol: 3mg
- Carbohydrates: 3g
- Dietary Fiber: 0g
- Sugars: 2g
- Protein: 46g

Tofu & Quinoa Bowl

Preparation Time: 30 minutes
Cooking Time: 40 minutes
Servings: 6

Ingredients:

- 15 oz. tofu, sliced into cubes
- 1 tablespoon sesame oil
- 1 tablespoon reduced-sodium soy sauce
- 6 cups cooked quinoa
- 1 cup carrots, shredded
- ½ cup cilantro, chopped
- ¼ cup scallions, chopped
- ½ cup slivered almonds

Sauce

- 1 clove garlic, minced
- 1 teaspoon ginger, grated
- 2 teaspoons peanut butter
- 3 tablespoons coconut milk
- 2 tablespoons rice wine vinegar
- 2 tablespoons hot sauce
- ½ tablespoon brown sugar
- 1 tablespoon lime juice

Method:

1. Preheat your oven to 350 degrees F.
2. In a bowl, toss the tofu in oil and soy sauce.
3. Spread tofu in your baking pan.
4. Bake for 40 minutes.
5. Add tofu, quinoa, carrots, cilantro, scallions and almonds to food containers.
6. Refrigerate for up to 2 days.
7. Reheat before serving.
8. In a bowl, mix the sauce ingredients.
9. Transfer to a sauce cup and refrigerate until ready to serve.

10. Reheat before drizzling on top of the tofu, quinoa and veggies.

Nutritional Content:

- Calories: 232
- Fat: 10 g
- Cholesterol: 0 mg
- Carbohydrates: 27 g
- Fiber: 4.5 g
- Sugars: 4 g
- Protein: 12 g

Asian-Style Pork Tenderloin

Preparation Time: 2 hours and 10 minutes
Cooking Time: 6 hours
Servings: 8

Ingredients:

Marinade

- 4 cloves garlic, minced
- 1 tablespoon ginger
- ¼ cup brown sugar
- ¼ cup reduced-sodium soy sauce
- 2 tablespoons rice vinegar
- 2 tablespoons lemon juice
- 1 tablespoon dry mustard
- 2 tablespoons Worcestershire sauce
- Pepper to taste

Pork

- 2 lb. pork tenderloin sliced into thin strips

Method:

1. Add all marinade ingredients to a bowl.
2. Mix well.
3. Soak the pork in the marinade.
4. Cover and refrigerate for 2 hours or transfer to sealable plastic bags and freeze for up to 2 months.
5. When ready to cook, cook in the slow cooker for 6 hours.

Nutritional Content:

- Calories: 256
- Fat: 9g
- Cholesterol: 5mg
- Carbohydrates: 9g
- Fiber: 0g
- Sugars: 8g
- Sodium: 658 mg
- Protein: 34g

Baked Chicken & Vegetables

Preparation Time: 20 minutes
Cooking Time: 1 hour
Servings: 6

Ingredients:

- 1 onion, sliced into wedges
- 6 carrots, sliced
- 4 potatoes, sliced
- 6 chicken breast fillets, sliced into cubes
- 1 teaspoon thyme
- Pepper to taste
- ½ cup water

Method:

1. Preheat your oven to 400 degrees F.
2. Toss onion, carrots and potatoes in a baking pan.
3. Arrange chicken on top.
4. In a bowl, combine thyme, pepper and water.
5. Pour on top of the chicken.
6. Bake in the oven for 1 hour.
7. Let cool.
8. Transfer to food container.
9. Refrigerate for up to 2 days.
10. Reheat before serving.

Nutritional Content:

- Calories: 240
- Cholesterol: 13mg
- Carbohydrate: 25 g
- Sugar: 10 g
- Fat: 3.5 g
- Sodium: 130 mg
- Fiber: 4 g
- Protein: 26 g

Ginger Beef Stir Fry

Preparation Time: 15 minutes
Cooking Time: 10 minutes
Servings: 6

Ingredients:

- 1 lb. flank steak, sliced into strips
- 2 cloves garlic, minced
- 2 teaspoons ground ginger
- 6 oz. nonfat beef broth
- 1 tablespoons cornstarch
- 3 tablespoons low-sodium soy sauce
- ¼ cup hoisin sauce
- 1 teaspoon canola oil
- ¼ teaspoon red pepper flakes
- 1 red bell pepper, sliced into strips
- 3 oz. broccoli florets

Method:

1. Season steak with garlic and ginger. Set aside.
2. In a bowl, mix broth, cornstarch, soy sauce and hoisin sauce. Mix well.
3. Pour oil into a pan over medium heat.
4. Add red pepper flakes.
5. Cook beef strips for 5 minutes, stirring often.
6. Add bell pepper and broccoli.
7. Cook for 2 minutes.
8. Add broth mixture.
9. Cook for 2 minutes.
10. Let cool.
11. Transfer to food containers.
12. Refrigerate for up to 3 days.
13. Reheat before serving.
14. Serve with brown rice.

Nutritional Content:

- Calories: 275
- Fat: 8 g
- Carbohydrates: 25 g
- Dietary Fiber: 2 g
- Sugars: 6 g
- Protein: 17 g

Barbecue Salmon

Preparation Time: 15 minutes
Cooking Time: 15 minutes
Servings: 4

Ingredients:

- 2 tablespoons lemon juice
- ¼ cup pineapple juice
- 4 salmon fillets
- 4 teaspoons chili powder
- 2 tablespoons brown sugar
- ¾ teaspoon ground cumin
- 2 teaspoons lemon zest
- ¼ teaspoon cinnamon

Method:

1. Preheat your oven to 400 degrees.
2. Mix lemon juice and pineapple juice in a sealable plastic bag.
3. Add salmon fillets.
4. Chill in the refrigerator for 1 hour.
5. Mix remaining ingredients.
6. Sprinkle fish with the mixture.
7. Bake in the oven for 15 minutes.
8. Transfer to food container and refrigerate for up to 3 days.
9. Reheat in the oven before serving.

Nutritional Content:

- Calories: 225
- Fat: 6 g
- Cholesterol: 88 mg
- Carbohydrate: 7 g
- Sodium: 407 mg
- Sugar: 6 g
- Protein: 34 g

Pork & Black Bean Stew

Preparation Time: 10 minutes
Cooking Time: 1 hour and 15 minutes
Servings: 4

Ingredients:

- 2 teaspoons olive oil
- 1 lb. lean pork loin or tenderloin, sliced into cubes
- 1 cup onion, chopped
- 3 cloves garlic, minced
- 2 cups canned chipotle peppers in adobo sauce, minced
- Garlic powder to taste
- 1 teaspoon ground cumin
- 14 oz. unsalted chicken broth
- 14 oz. low-sodium canned black beans, rinsed and drained
- 14 oz. low-sodium canned diced tomatoes

Method:

1. Add oil to a pan over medium high heat.
2. Cook pork cubes until golden on all sides.
3. Add onion, garlic, chipotle peppers, garlic powder and cumin.
4. Cook for 2 to 3 minutes, stirring.
5. Pour in broth, beans and tomatoes.
6. Bring to a boil.
7. Reduce heat and simmer for 1 hour.

Nutritional Content:

- Calories: 308
- Fat: 7 g
- Cholesterol: 84 mg
- Carbohydrate: 25 g
- Sodium: 414 mg
- Fiber: 6 g
- Protein: 33 g

Fried Trout

Preparation Time: 15 minutes
Cooking Time: 10 minutes
Servings: 2

Ingredients:

- 3 tablespoons yellow cornmeal
- ¼ teaspoon ground celery seeds
- 2 tablespoons parsley, chopped
- Pepper to taste
- 2 rainbow trout fillets
- 2 teaspoons olive oil

Method:

1. In a bowl, combine cornmeal, ground celery, parsley and pepper.
2. Coat both sides of the fish with this mixture.
3. Transfer breaded fish to a food container.
4. Freeze for up to 1 month.
5. When ready to cook, add olive oil to a pan over medium heat.
6. Cook in the pan for 3 to 5 minutes per side or until crispy.

Nutritional Content:

- Calories: 240
- Fat: 10g
- Cholesterol: 67mg
- Carbohydrates: 10g
- Sodium: 338mg
- Sugars: 0g
- Protein: 25g

Cajun Chicken

Preparation Time: 30 minutes
Cooking Time: 1 hour
Servings: 4

Ingredients:

- 1 lb. chicken breast fillets
- 1 cup spinach, cooked and drained
- 3 oz. low-fat pepper Jack cheese, shredded
- 1 tablespoon breadcrumbs
- 2 tablespoons Cajun seasoning
- 2 teaspoons olive oil

Method:

1. Flatten chicken with a meat mallet.
2. In a bowl, mix spinach and cheese.
3. In another bowl, mix breadcrumbs and seasoning.
4. Spread spinach mixture on top of chicken breast and roll them up.
5. Brush chicken with oil and coat with seasoned breadcrumbs.
6. Wrap each rolled chicken with foil or plastic wrap.
7. Freeze for up to 1 week.
8. When ready to cook, place in a baking pan.
9. Bake at 350 degrees F for 50 minutes to 1 hour.

Nutritional Content:

- Calories: 241
- Fat: 9.7g
- Carbohydrates: 2g
- Dietary Fiber: 1g
- Sugars: 0g
- Protein: 32g

Creamy Chicken

Preparation Time: 20 minutes
Cooking Time: 4 hours
Servings: 6

Ingredients:

- Cooking spray
- 6 chicken breast fillets
- ½ cup chicken stock
- 11 oz. low-fat cream of mushroom soup
- 1 cup plain Greek yogurt
- 8 oz. mushrooms
- 1 packet Italian dressing mix

Method:

1. Spray your pan with oil.
2. Place it over medium heat.
3. Cook chicken until brown on both sides.
4. Transfer to a slow cooker.
5. Stir in the rest of the ingredients.
6. Cover the pot.
7. Cook on low for 4 hours.

Nutritional Content:

- Calories: 128
- Fat: 1.68 g
- Cholesterol: 90mg
- Sugar: 2.28 g
- Sodium: 257mg
- Protein: 18.5 g

Chicken Tikka Masala

Preparation Time: 20 minutes
Cooking Time: 8 hours
Servings: 10

Ingredients:

- 2 tablespoons olive oil
- 1 onion, diced
- 4 cloves garlic, minced
- 2 tablespoons ginger, minced
- 3 lb. chicken breast fillets, sliced into strips
- 1 ½ cups Greek yogurt
- 29 oz. canned tomato puree
- 1 tablespoon cumin
- 2 tablespoons garam masala
- ¾ teaspoon cinnamon
- ½ tablespoon paprika
- 2 bay leaves
- Pepper to taste

Method:

1. Add all ingredients to a bowl.
2. Mix well.
3. Transfer to a slow cooker.
4. Cover the pot.
5. Cook for 8 hours on low.
6. Discard bay leaves.
7. Let cool.
8. Transfer to food containers.
9. Freeze for up to 1 month.
10. Reheat before serving.

Nutritional Content:

- Calories: 270
- Fat: 8 g
- Cholesterol: 20 mg
- Sodium: 151 mg

- Carbohydrates: 12 g
- Fiber: 2 g
- Sugars: 7 g
- Protein: 45 g

Crispy Tuna Patties

Preparation Time: 15 minutes
Cooking Time: 6 minutes
Servings: 8

Ingredients:

- 12 oz. canned tuna flakes
- 4 egg whites
- 16 wheat crackers, crushed
- ¼ cup carrot, grated
- ¼ cup capers, diced
- 1 tablespoon onion, minced
- Dried mustard to taste
- Cooking spray

Method:

1. Combine ingredients in a bowl.
2. Form patties from the mixture.
3. Wrap patties with cling wrap or foil.
4. Freeze for up to 1 month.
5. When ready to cook, spray your pan with oil.
6. Place it over medium heat.
7. Cook patties for 3 minutes per side.
8. Serve immediately.

Nutritional Content:

- Calories: 80 calories
- Fat: 1 gram
- Cholesterol: 22 g
- Carbohydrate: 4 g
- Sodium: 240 mg
- Sugar: 0 g
- Protein: 12 g

Sweet & Sour Pork

Preparation Time: 15 minutes
Cooking Time: 40 minutes
Servings: 6

Ingredients:

- Cooking spray
- 1 lb. lean pork tenderloin, sliced into strips
- ¼ cup pineapple juice
- ¼ cup Splenda sweetener
- ½ cup water
- 2 tablespoons cornstarch
- 1 tablespoon reduced-sodium soy sauce
- Salt to taste
- 1 onion, sliced
- 1 red bell pepper, sliced
- 15 oz. pineapple chunks
- ¼ cup rice vinegar

Method:

1. Spray your pan with oil.
2. Place it over medium high heat.
3. Cook pork until golden on both sides.
4. Transfer to a plate.
5. Remove fat from the pan.
6. In a bowl, mix the pineapple juice, sweetener, water, cornstarch, soy sauce and salt.
7. Add to the pan.
8. Cook for 2 minutes.
9. Put pork back to the pan.
10. Cook for 30 minutes.
11. Add remaining ingredients.
12. Cook for 5 minutes.

Nutritional Content:

- Calories: 248
- Fat: 3.5 g

- Cholesterol: 60 mg
- Carbohydrate: 36 g
- Sodium: 354 mg
- Sugar: 8 g
- Protein: 18 g

Crispy Chicken

Preparation Time: 1 hour and 20 minutes
Cooking Time: 30 minutes
Servings: 3

Ingredients:

- ¼ cup low-fat buttermilk
- ⅛ tsp. paprika
- 12 oz. chicken breast tenders
- ¼ cup bran cereal
- 1 tablespoon dry onion soup mix
- ¼ cup panko breadcrumbs

Method:

1. Mix milk and paprika in a bowl.
2. Put chicken in the bowl.
3. Coat with the mixture.
4. Cover and refrigerate for 1 hour.
5. Add cereal to a food processor.
6. Pulse until fully ground.
7. Mix ground cereal with onion soup mix and breadcrumbs.
8. Coat chicken with the breadcrumb mixture.
9. Place in a food container.
10. Freeze for up to 2 weeks.
11. When ready to cook, bake in the oven at 375 degrees F for 15 minutes per side.

Nutritional Content:

- Calories: 210
- Fat: 3.5g
- Cholesterol: 2 mg
- Carbohydrates: 17g
- Fiber: 3.5g
- Sugar: 2g
- Protein: 29g

Chicken Casserole

Preparation Time: 30 minutes
Cooking Time: 30 minutes
Servings: 4

Ingredients:

- 2 cups frozen mixed veggies
- 1 cup whole wheat pasta, cooked
- 1 cup chicken breast, cooked and sliced into cubes
- 10 ½ oz. nonfat cream of chicken soup
- 1 cup low-fat cheddar cheese, shredded
- 4 oz. mushrooms
- ¾ cup water
- Onion powder to taste

Method:

1. Spray your casserole dish with oil.
2. In a pan over medium heat, cook frozen veggies according to directions.
3. In a bowl, mix cooked veggies, cooked pasta and remaining ingredients.
4. Pour mixture into a casserole dish.
5. Cover and refrigerate for up to 1 day.
6. When ready to cook, bake in the oven at 350 degrees F for 30 minutes.

Nutritional Content:

- Calories: 256
- Fat: 8 g
- Cholesterol: 12 mg
- Carbohydrate: 27 g
- Sodium: 834 mg
- Sugar: 3 g
- Protein: 19 g

Chapter 7: Snacks

Chicken & Cheese Steak Wrap

Preparation Time: 10 minutes
Cooking Time: 7 minutes
Serving: 1

Ingredients:

- Cooking spray
- ¼ cup onion, chopped
- ¼ lb. chicken breast fillet, sliced into thin strips
- ¼ cup green bell pepper, chopped
- ¼ cup mushrooms, sliced
- ¾ cup Swiss cheese
- 1 whole wheat flour

Method:

1. Spray your pan with oil.
2. Add onion and chicken.
3. Cook for 3 to 5 minutes.
4. Stir in bell pepper and mushrooms for 2 minutes.
5. Let cool.
6. Transfer to food container.
7. When ready to serve, reheat mixture.
8. Add mixture and cheese on top of the tortilla.
9. Roll up and serve.

Nutritional Content:

- Calories: 264
- Carbohydrate: 17 g
- Fat: 6 g
- Protein: 33 g
- Cholesterol: 76 mg
- Sodium: 620 mg
- Fiber: 4 g

Pesto Pasta

Preparation Time: 15 minutes
Cooking Time: 0 minute
Servings: 4

Ingredients:

- 1 tablespoon olive oil
- ½ cup water
- ¼ cup fresh basil leaves
- 2 cloves garlic, minced
- 10 oz. spinach, chopped
- 2 tablespoons Parmesan cheese, grated
- 4 cups cooked whole wheat pasta

Method:

1. Add all ingredients except to a food processor.
2. Pulse until smooth.
3. Refrigerate pesto sauce for up to 5 days.
4. When ready to serve, toss cooked pasta in sauce and serve.

Nutritional Content:

- Calories: 77
- Fat: 5 g
- Cholesterol: 3 mg
- Carbohydrate: 4 gram
- Sodium: 292 mg
- Sugar: 1 gram
- Protein: 6 g

Chicken Caprese

Preparation Time: 5 minutes
Cooking Time: 6 minutes
Servings: 4

Ingredients:

- 1 lb. chicken breast fillet
- 1 tablespoon olive oil
- Pepper to taste
- 1 teaspoon Italian seasoning
- 1 tomato, sliced thickly
- 4 mozzarella cheese slices
- 3 tablespoons balsamic vinegar
- 2 tablespoons basil, sliced thinly

Method:

1. Drizzle chicken with oil.
2. Season with pepper and Italian seasoning.
3. Heat a grill or grill pan over medium high heat.
4. Grill chicken for 3 minutes per side.
5. Let cool.
6. Transfer to food containers.
7. When ready to serve, reheat on the grill.
8. Top with the remaining ingredients and serve.

Nutritional Content:

- Calories: 230
- Fat: 9 gram
- Cholesterol: 80 mg
- Sodium: 105 mg
- Carbohydrates: 4 g
- Dietary Fiber: 0 g
- Sugar: 2.5 g
- Protein: 33 g

Turkey Turnover

Preparation Time: 10 minutes
Cooking Time: 15 minutes
Servings: 24

Ingredients:

- 1 cup low-fat cheese, shredded
- 1 lb. ground turkey
- 1 packet dry onion soup
- 3 tubes low-fat refrigerated crescent rolls

Method:

1. Combine cheese, ground turkey and onion soup mix in a pan over medium heat.
2. Separate rolls and slice in triangle.
3. Spread mixture on top of the triangles.
4. Fold over and seal the edges.
5. Freeze until ready to serve.
6. When ready to cook, bake in the oven at 350 degrees F for 15 minutes.

Nutritional Content:

- Calories: 155
- Fat: 7 g
- Cholesterol: 14 mg
- Carbohydrate: 13 g
- Sodium: 472 mg
- Sugar: 3 g
- Protein: 9 g

Chicken Wrap

Preparation Time: 15 minutes
Cooking Time: 15 minutes
Servings: 4

Ingredients:

Sauce

- 8 oz. water chestnuts, minced
- 8 oz. bamboo shoots, minced
- 2 tablespoons hoisin sauce
- 3 tablespoons sherry cooking wine
- 2 packets Splenda sweetener
- 2 teaspoons reduced-sodium soy sauce
- 1 tablespoon no-salt peanut butter
- 2 teaspoons hot pepper sauce

Chicken

- 1 teaspoon olive oil
- 1 tablespoon garlic, minced
- 1 cup onion, minced
- 1 teaspoon ginger, minced
- ½ lb. ground chicken breast
- 8 large lettuce leaves
- 1 cucumber, sliced into strips

Method:

1. Mix sauce ingredients in a bowl. Set aside.
2. Add oil to a pan over medium heat.
3. Cook onion and garlic for 5 minutes.
4. Add ginger and chicken.
5. Cook for 4 minutes.
6. Stir in sauce mixture.
7. Cook for 2 to 4 minutes.
8. Turn off heat.
9. Let cool.

10. Transfer to food containers.
11. Refrigerate for up to 2 days.
12. When ready to serve, reheat mixture.
13. Top lettuce with the mixture and with cucumber strips.
14. Roll them up and serve.

Nutritional Content:

- Calories: 155
- Fat: 4 g
- Cholesterol: 33 mg
- Carbohydrates: 11 g
- Sodium: 637 mg
- Dietary Fiber: 5 g
- Sugar: 4 g
- Protein: 16 g

Chicken Rolls

Preparation Time: 30 minutes
Cooking Time: 30 minutes
Servings: 8

Ingredients:

- 8 chicken breasts, sliced into cubes
- ½ cup Italian seasoned breadcrumbs
- ¼ cup parmesan cheese, grated
- 6 tablespoons egg whites
- 5 oz. spinach, cooked
- 6 tablespoons ricotta cheese
- 6 oz. low-fat and unsalted mozzarella, shredded
- 1 cup marinara sauce

Method:

1. Sprinkle chicken with salt and pepper.
2. In a bowl, mix breadcrumbs with Parmesan cheese.
3. Add egg whites to another bowl.
4. In another bowl, mix mozzarella with spinach and ricotta cheese.
5. Top each chicken with the mozzarella mixture.
6. Roll them up.
7. Soak in egg whites and coat with breadcrumbs.
8. Arrange in a single layer in a food container.
9. Freeze for up to 1 month.
10. When ready to cook, bake in the oven at 450 degrees for 20 to 30 minutes.
11. Top with marinara sauce and serve.

Nutritional Content:

- Calories: 268
- Fat: 9 g
- Cholesterol: 0 mg
- Carbohydrates: 8 g
- Fiber: 1.5 g
- Sugars: 3 g
- Protein: 36 g

Veggie Pizza

Preparation Time: 20 minutes
Cooking Time: 20 minutes
Servings: 8

Ingredients:

- ¼ cup dry ranch dressing mix
- ½ cup light sour cream
- ½ cup low-fat onion and chive cream cheese
- 2 low-carb tortilla wraps
- ¾ cup tomatoes, diced
- ¾ cup broccoli florets
- ⅛ cup green bell pepper, diced
- ⅛ cup carrots, shredded
- ⅛ cup cucumbers, diced
- ½ cup black olives, sliced
- ¾ cup Monterey Jack cheese, shredded

Method:

1. Combine ranch dressing mix, sour cream and cream cheese.
2. Spread mixture on top of tortillas.
3. Top with vegetables and cheese.
4. Cover with foil or plastic wrap.
5. Freeze for up to 1 week.
6. When ready to cook, bake in the oven at 350 degrees F for 20 minutes.

Nutritional Content:

- Calories: 170
- Fat: 10 g
- Protein: 10 g
- Carbohydrate: 12 g
- Cholesterol: 23 mg
- Sodium: 870 mg
- Sugar: 1.6 g
- Fiber: 4 g

Stuffed Acorn Squash

Preparation Time: 10 minutes
Cooking Time: 20 minutes
Servings: 4

Ingredients:

- 2 acorn squash, sliced in half and seeds removed
- 1 cup onion, chopped
- 1 cup celery, diced
- 1 cup mushrooms, sliced
- 1 lb. lean ground turkey
- 1 teaspoon basil
- 1 teaspoon oregano
- 1 teaspoon garlic powder
- Salt and pepper to taste
- 8 oz. canned tomato sauce
- 1 cup low-fat cheddar cheese, shredded

Method:

1. Preheat your oven to 350 degrees F.
2. Bake the squash in the oven for 40 minutes.
3. In a pan over medium heat, cook onion, celery, mushrooms and turkey for 5 minutes.
4. Season with herbs, spices, salt and pepper.
5. Add tomato sauce.
6. Refrigerate squash and sauce mixture in separate containers.
7. When ready to cook, top squash with sauce mixture and cheese.
8. Bake in the oven at 350 degrees F for 15 minutes.

Nutritional Content:

- Calories: 299
- Fat: 4 g
- Carbohydrates: 38g
- Fiber: 6g
- Sugars: 9g
- Protein: 30g

Zucchini Boats

Preparation Time: 20 minutes
Cooking Time: 30 minutes
Servings: 8

Ingredients:

- 4 zucchinis, sliced in half and flesh scooped out
- 1 lb. ground turkey breast
- ½ white onion, chopped
- 1 egg, beaten
- 1 tomato, diced
- ½ lb. mushrooms, sliced
- ¼ cup whole wheat breadcrumbs
- ¾ cup spaghetti sauce
- Salt and pepper to taste
- 1 cup low fat mozzarella cheese, shredded

Method:

1. Microwave zucchini halves for 3 minutes.
2. Drain. Set aside.
3. In a pan over medium heat, cook onion and ground turkey for 3 to 5 minutes.
4. In a bowl, mix turkey mixture with the rest of the ingredients except cheese.
5. Spread mixture on top of zucchini boats.
6. Top with cheese.
7. Cover with foil and refrigerate for up to 1 day.
8. When ready to cook, bake in the oven at 350 degrees F for 20 minutes.

Nutritional Content:

- Calories: 195
- Fat: 7.5g
- Cholesterol: 0 mg
- Sodium: 294 mg
- Carbohydrates: 16g
- Fiber: 4g
- Sugars: 5g
- Protein: 17.5g

Stuffed French Toast

Preparation Time: 10 minutes
Cooking Time: 5 minutes
Servings: 1

Ingredients:

- ½ cup ricotta cheese
- 4 slices bread
- 2 packets sugar substitute
- 3 egg whites, beaten
- ¼ teaspoon vanilla extract
- ¼ teaspoon pumpkin pie spice
- Cooking spray

Method:

1. Spread ricotta on top of 2 bread slices.
2. Sprinkle with sugar
3. Add 2 bread slices on top to make sandwich.
4. Mix egg white, vanilla extract and pumpkin pie spice.
5. Dip bread in egg white mixture.
6. Freeze until ready to cook.
7. When ready to cook, fry in a pan misted with oil until golden.

Nutritional Content:

- Calories: 227
- Fat: .5 g
- Cholesterol: 20 mg
- Carbohydrate: 27 g
- Sodium: 659 mg
- Sugar: 8 g
- Protein: 25 g

Chapter 8: Desserts

Pumpkin Mousse

Preparation Time: 5 minutes
Cooking Time: 0 minute
Servings: 4

Ingredients:

- 15 oz. pumpkin puree
- 2 cups whipped topping (sugar free)
- ½ cup skim milk
- 1 teaspoon cinnamon
- Pinch nutmeg

Method:

1. In a bowl, combine all ingredients.
2. Mix until creamy.
3. Transfer to glass jars with lids.
4. Refrigerate for up to 3 days.

Nutritional Content:

- Calories: 149
- Fat: 4.4 g
- Protein: 2 g
- Carbohydrate: 28 g
- Cholesterol: 0 mg
- Sodium: 71 mg
- Sugar: 8.6 g
- Fiber: 3.4 g

Brownie Bites

Preparation Time: 15 minutes
Cooking Time: 10 minutes
Servings: 4

Ingredients:

- 2 eggs
- 1 avocado, sliced
- 3 tablespoons butter
- ½ Splenda
- ½ teaspoon vanilla extract
- ¼ cup dark chocolate chips
- ½ cup cocoa powder
- ½ teaspoon salt
- ½ cup almond flour
- 1 teaspoon baking soda

Method:

1. Preheat your oven to 350 degrees F.
2. Add eggs, avocado, butter, Splenda and vanilla extract to a food processor.
3. Pulse until smooth.
4. Transfer to a bowl.
5. Add the remaining ingredients.
6. Pour mixture into a muffin pan.
7. Bake in the oven for 10 minutes.
8. Let cool.
9. Transfer to airtight container.
10. Refrigerate for up to 1 week.

Nutritional Content:

- Calories: 150
- Fat: 5 g
- Cholesterol: 0 mg
- Sodium: 15 mg
- Carbohydrates: 22 g
- Fiber: 3 g
- Sugar: 4 g
- Protein: 6 g

Silky Fudge Dessert

Preparation Time: 40 minutes
Cooking Time: 0 minute
Servings: 8

Ingredients:

- 1 packed unflavored gelatin
- ¼ cup hot water
- 1.4 oz. instant pudding mix (sugar and fat free)
- 1 cup cold skim milk
- 16 oz. silken tofu, diced
- ½ teaspoon vanilla extract

Method:

1. Combine gelatin and hot water.
2. Let the mixture become firm.
3. In another bowl, blend the pudding mix and milk.
4. Add tofu to the pudding mixture.
5. Stir in vanilla extract.
6. Add tofu mixture to a food processor.
7. Pulse until smooth.
8. Add gelatin and stir.
9. Pour into a baking pan.
10. Refrigerate for 30 minutes.
11. Transfer to food containers and refrigerate for up to 3 days.

Nutritional Content:

- Calories: 56
- Fat: 1 g
- Cholesterol: 1 mg
- Carbohydrate: 6 g
- Sodium: 181 mg
- Fiber: 0 g
- Protein: 5 g

Dessert Cups

Preparation Time: 5 minutes
Cooking Time: 3 minutes
Servings: 18

Ingredients:

- ¼ teaspoon coconut oil, melted
- ½ cup coconut butter, softened
- 2 cups chocolate chips (sugar free)

Method:

1. Line your muffin tin with liners.
2. Mix all ingredients in a bowl.
3. Pour mixture into muffin cups.
4. Freeze until ready to serve.

Nutritional Content:

- Calories: 120
- Fat: 8 g
- Cholesterol: 10 mg
- Sodium: 1 mg
- Carbohydrates: 6 g
- Fiber: 4 g
- Sugar: 1 g
- Protein: 1 g

Cheesecake Pudding

Preparation Time: 5 minutes
Cooking Time: 0 minute
Servings: 1

Ingredients:

- 1 cup nonfat plain Greek yogurt
- 1 package cheesecake pudding mix (sugar-free)

Method:

1. Add yogurt and pudding mix to a food processor.
2. Pulse until smooth.
3. Transfer to food containers.
4. Refrigerate for up to 3 days.

Nutritional Content:

- Calories: 31
- Carbohydrate: 5 g
- Fat: 2 g (0 g saturated)
- Protein: 6 g
- Cholesterol: 1 mg
- Sodium: 105 mg
- Fiber: 0 g

Jello

Preparation Time: 5 minutes
Cooking Time: 0 minute
Servings: 4

Ingredients:

- 1 box jello (sugar-free)
- 8 tablespoons whipped topping (sugar free)

Method:

1. Follow package directions for making jello.
2. Refrigerate until set.
3. Divide jello into 4 glass jars with lid.
4. Top with the whipped topping.
5. Refrigerate for up to 3 days.

Nutritional Content:

- Calories: 30
- Fat: 0 g
- Cholesterol: 0 mg
- Carbohydrate: 2 g
- Sodium: 65 mg
- Sugar: 1 g
- Protein: 1 gram

Cream Cheese Cookies

Preparation Time: 10 minutes
Cooking Time: 15 minutes
Servings: 24

Ingredients:

- 3 cups almond flour
- 2 oz. cream cheese
- ¼ cup butter, softened
- 1 egg, beaten
- 1/3 cup monk fruit blend
- 2 teaspoons vanilla extract
- 1 teaspoon Splenda
- Pinch salt

Method:

1. Combine all ingredients in a bowl.
2. Form cookies from the mixture.
3. Bake at 350 degrees for 15 minutes.
4. Let cool.
5. Transfer to airtight container.
6. Refrigerate for up to 1 week.

Nutritional Content:

- Calories: 110
- Fat: 10g
- Cholesterol: 10mg
- Carbohydrate: 3g
- Fiber: 2g
- Sugar: 1g
- Protein: 3g

Spinach & Strawberry Salad

Preparation Time: 10 minutes
Cooking Time: 0 minute
Servings: 4

Ingredients:

- 10 oz. spinach, sliced
- 1 qt. strawberries, sliced
- ¼ cup almonds, slivered

Dressing

- ½ cup olive oil
- ¼ cup white vinegar
- 1 tablespoon onion, minced
- 1 tablespoon poppy seeds
- 2 tablespoons sesame seeds
- ¼ teaspoon Worcestershire sauce
- ¼ teaspoon paprika

Method:

1. Arrange spinach in food containers.
2. Top with strawberries and almonds.
3. Mix dressing ingredients in a glass jar with lid.
4. Shake to blend well.
5. Refrigerate salad and dressing for up to 2 days.
6. Pour dressing over salad when ready to serve.

Nutritional Content:

- Calories: 490
- Fat: 35.2

Chocolate Mousse

Preparation Time: 5 minutes
Cooking Time: 0 minute
Servings: 4

Ingredients:

- 1/8 cup cocoa powder
- 4 oz. cream cheese (fat free)
- 2 tablespoons almond milk (unsweetened)
- 1 teaspoon vanilla extract
- ¼ cup honey
- ¾ cup light whipped topping

Method:

1. Use a hand mixer to mix ingredients except whipped topping.
2. Stir in the whipped topping.
3. Transfer to glass jars with lid.
4. Refrigerate until ready to serve or for up to 3 days.

Nutritional Content:

- Calories: 63
- Fat: 2 g
- Cholesterol: 10 mg
- Sodium: 102 mg
- Carbohydrates: 7 g
- Fiber: 3 g
- Sugar: 2 g
- Protein: 4 g

Chocolate Chip Cookies

Preparation Time: 10 minutes
Cooking Time: 12 minutes
Servings: 12

Ingredients:

- ½ cup butter, melted
- ¾ cup Splenda
- 1 egg, beaten
- 1 teaspoon vanilla extract
- 1 ½ cups almond flour
- ¼ teaspoon salt
- ½ teaspoon baking powder
- ¾ cup chocolate chips (sugar-free)

Method:

1. Preheat your oven to 350 degrees F.
2. Mix butter and Splenda in a bowl.
3. Stir in egg and vanilla.
4. Add the remaining ingredients.
5. Mix well.
6. Form cookies from the mixture.
7. Bake in the oven for 10 to 12 minutes.
8. Let cool.
9. Transfer to airtight container.
10. Refrigerate for up to 1 week.

Nutritional Content:

- Calories: 135
- Fat: 6 g
- Cholesterol: 3 mg
- Sodium: 27 mg
- Carbohydrates: 20 g
- Fiber: 2 g
- Sugar: 2 g
- Protein: 5 g

Pudding Bites

Preparation Time: 5 minutes
Cooking Time: 5 minutes
Servings: 1

Ingredients:

- 2 tablespoons Splenda
- 1 cup skim milk
- 3 cups low-sugar chocolate chips
- ½ teaspoon vanilla extract

Method:

1. Mix the Splenda and milk in a pan over medium heat.
2. Cook while stirring for 1 minute.
3. Stir in the baking chips.
4. Add vanilla extract and turn off heat.
5. Transfer to glass jars with lid.
6. Refrigerate until ready to serve or for up to 3 days.

Nutritional Content:

- Calories: 142
- Fat: 7.2 g
- Cholesterol: 0 mg
- Sodium: 0 mg
- Carbohydrates: 20.4 g
- Fiber: 0 g
- Sugar: 6.4 g
- Protein: 5.6 g

Chapter 9: Salads

Green Salad

Preparation Time: 10 minutes
Cooking Time: 0 minute
Servings: 4

Ingredients:

Salad

- 4 cups mixed salad greens
- 1 avocado, sliced into cubes
- ½ cup almonds, sliced

Dressing

- 4 tablespoons olive oil
- 1 tablespoon Dijon mustard
- 2 cloves garlic, minced
- 1 teaspoon fresh parsley, chopped
- 1/8 teaspoon Splenda
- 2 tablespoons white wine vinegar
- 1 teaspoon lemon juice
- Salt and pepper to taste

Method:

1. Arrange salad greens in food containers.
2. Top with avocado and almonds.
3. Seal and refrigerate for up to 3 days.
4. Combine dressing in a separate container.
5. Refrigerate until ready to serve.
6. Drizzle with dressing before serving.

Nutritional Content:

- Calories: 325
- Fat: 15 g
- Cholesterol: 12.6 mg
- Sodium: 561 mg

- Carbohydrates: 10.5 g
- Fiber: 5.9 g
- Sugar: 1.8 g
- Protein: 6.5 g

Summer Salad

Preparation Time: 15 minutes
Cooking Time: 0 minute
Servings: 4

Ingredients:

- 4 cups Romaine lettuce
- 1 apple, diced
- 1 pear, diced
- ¼ cup dried cranberries
- ¼ cup Swiss cheese, shredded
- ¼ cup cashews

Dressing

- ¼ cup olive oil
- ¼ cup orange juice
- 1 teaspoon onion, minced
- 1 tablespoon Splenda
- 1 tablespoon poppy seeds
- Pinch salt

Method:

1. Arrange Romaine lettuce in food containers.
2. Sprinkle fruits, cheese and cashews on top.
3. Seal the food container.
4. Refrigerate for up to 1 day.
5. Mix dressing ingredients in a sauce cup or glass jar with lid.
6. Drizzle salad with dressing when ready to serve.

Nutritional Content:

- Calories: 314
- Fat: 24.4 g
- Cholesterol: 9 mg
- Sodium: 342 mg
- Carbohydrates: 21.3 g
- Fiber: 1.8 g
- Sugar: 4 g
- Protein: 5.5 g

Roasted Beet Salad

Preparation Time: 10 minutes
Cooking Time: 50 minutes
Servings: 4

Ingredients:

- 2 beets, trimmed
- 2 tablespoons balsamic vinegar
- 2 teaspoons maple syrup
- Salt and pepper to taste

Method:

1. Preheat your oven to 400 degrees F.
2. Wrap beets with foil.
3. Add to a baking pan.
4. Roast in the oven for 50 minutes.
5. Unwrap and let cool. Peel and slice the beets.
6. Mix remaining ingredients in a bowl.
7. Pour mixture over the beets.
8. Transfer to food containers.
9. Refrigerate for up to 2 days.

Nutritional Content:

- Calories: 66
- Fat: 0.2 g
- Cholesterol: 0 mg
- Sodium: 135 mg
- Carbohydrates: 15 g
- Fiber: 3.4 g
- Sugar: 4 g
- Protein: 2 g

Carrot & Cucumber Salad

Preparation Time: 15 minutes
Cooking Time: 0 minute
Servings: 2

Ingredients:

- 1 cup carrot, sliced
- ½ cucumber, sliced
- 2 tablespoons red bell pepper, minced
- 2 tablespoons green onion, chopped

Dressing

- ¼ cup rice vinegar
- 1 teaspoon Splenda
- ½ teaspoon olive oil
- ¼ teaspoon ginger, grated

Method:

1. Toss carrot, cucumber, red bell pepper and green onion in food containers.
2. Seal. Refrigerate for up to 2 days.
3. Mix dressing ingredients.
4. Store in glass jar with lid.
5. Refrigerate.
6. Pour dressing over salad when ready to serve.

Nutritional Content:

- Calories: 58
- Fat: 1.4 g
- Cholesterol: 0 mg
- Sodium: 35 mg
- Carbohydrates: 11 g
- Fiber: 2.4 g
- Sugar: 3 g
- Protein: 1.4 g

Cucumber Salad

Preparation Time: 10 minutes
Cooking Time: 0 minute
Servings: 4

Ingredients:

- 1 white onion, chopped
- 4 cucumbers, sliced thinly
- ½ cup water
- 1 cup white vinegar
- 2 tablespoons dried dill
- 1 tablespoon cup Splenda

Method:

1. Combine all ingredients in a bowl.
2. Divide into 4 food containers
3. Seal and refrigerate for up to 3 days.

Nutritional Content:

- Calories: 98
- Fat: 0.2 g
- Cholesterol: 0 mg
- Sodium: 4.4 mg
- Carbohydrates: 20 g
- Fiber: 1 g
- Sugar: 2 g
- Protein: 1 g

Spinach & Cranberry Salad

Preparation Time: 10 minutes
Cooking Time: 0 minute
Servings: 8

Ingredients:

- 1 lb. spinach, sliced
- 1 cup dried cranberries
- 2 tablespoons toasted sesame seeds
- ¾ cup almonds, slivered
- 1 tablespoon poppy seeds

Dressing

- ½ cup cider vinegar
- ½ cup olive oil
- 2 teaspoons onion, minced
- ¼ teaspoon paprika

Method:

1. Toss spinach and cranberries in food containers.
2. Top with the sesame seeds, almond and poppy seeds.
3. In a separate container, mix dressing ingredients.
4. Refrigerate for up to 3 days.
5. Drizzle dressing over the salad when ready to serve.

Nutritional Content:

- Calories: 338
- Fat: 23.5
- Cholesterol: 3.8 mg
- Sodium: 57 mg
- Carbohydrates: 30.4 g
- Fiber: 3.6 g
- Sugar: 23.2 g
- Protein: 4.9 g

Kale Salad

Preparation Time: 15 minutes
Cooking Time: 0 minute
Servings: 4

Ingredients:

- 6 cups kale leaves
- 1 cup croutons

Dressing

- ½ cup olive oil
- ½ cup lemon juice
- ½ teaspoon Dijon mustard
- 2 cloves garlic, minced

Method:

1. Place kale leaves in food containers.
2. Top with croutons.
3. Seal and refrigerate for up to 2 days.
4. Mix dressing ingredients and add to a sauce cup.
5. Refrigerate.
6. Drizzle salad with dressing before serving.

Nutritional Content:

- Calories: 361
- Fat: 13
- Cholesterol: 6 mg
- Sodium: 437 mg
- Carbohydrates: 17.6 g
- Fiber: 2.2 g
- Sugar: 1.2 g
- Protein: 6.8 g

Mediterranean Salad

Preparation Time: 10 minutes
Cooking Time: 0 minute
Servings: 4

Ingredients:

- 2 cucumbers, sliced
- ¼ cup sun-dried tomatoes, sliced
- 2 cups tomatoes, diced
- 1 red onion, sliced
- 1 cup black olives, sliced
- 1 ½ cup feta cheese, crumbled

Method:

1. Combine all ingredients in food containers.
2. Seal and refrigerate for up to 1 day.

Nutritional Content:

- Calories: 130
- Fat: 8.8
- Cholesterol: 25 mg
- Sodium: 86 mg
- Carbohydrates: 9.3 g
- Fiber: 2.1 g
- Sugar: 4.5 g
- Protein: 5.5 g
- Cholesterol: 0 mg
- Sodium: 62 mg
- Carbohydrates: 32 g
- Fiber: 6.2 g
- Sugar: 3 g
- Protein: 6 g

Broccoli Salad

Preparation Time: 15 minutes
Cooking Time: 0 minute
Servings: 4

Ingredients:

- 4 cups broccoli florets
- ½ cup almonds, sliced
- 1 cup raisins
- ½ onion, minced
- 1 cup mayonnaise
- 2 tablespoons white wine vinegar
- Pinch garlic salt

Method:

1. Mix all ingredients in food container.
2. Seal and refrigerate for up to 3 days.

Nutritional Content:

- Calories: 373.8
- Fat: 7 g
- Cholesterol: 13 mg
- Sodium: 35 mg
- Carbohydrates: 28 g
- Fiber: 3.2 g
- Sugar: 3 g
- Protein: 7.3 g

Chapter 10: Drinks

Spinach & Banana Smoothie

Preparation Time: 5 minutes
Cooking Time: 0 minute
Servings: 1

Ingredients:

- 1 banana, sliced
- 1 cup spinach leaves
- 1 cup unsweetened soymilk

Method:

1. Process all ingredients in a blender.
2. Chill in the refrigerator for up to 1 day.

Nutritional Content:

- Calories: 257.4
- Fat: 4.8
- Cholesterol: 0 mg
- Sodium: 14 mg
- Carbohydrates: 47.1 g
- Fiber: 5.5 g
- Sugar: 6 g
- Protein: 10.1 g

Blackberry Lemonade

Preparation Time: 5 minutes
Cooking Time: 0 minute
Servings: 4

Ingredients:

- 1 cup blackberries
- ¾ cup Splenda
- 4 ½ cups water
- 1 cup lemon juice
- 4 cups ice cubes

Method:

1. Blend blackberries in a food processor.
2. Add pureed blackberries and the rest of the ingredients to a pitcher.
3. Refrigerate for up to 2 days.

Nutritional Content:

- Calories: 200
- Fat: 0.2 g
- Cholesterol: 0 mg
- Sodium: 15 mg
- Carbohydrates: 52.5 g
- Fiber: 2 g
- Sugar: 4 g
- Protein: 0.7 g

Green Smoothie

Preparation Time: 5 minutes
Cooking Time: 0 minute
Servings: 2

Ingredients:

- 6 leaves kale
- 2 green apples, sliced
- 1 cucumber, sliced
- 4 stalks celery
- 1 tablespoon ginger, minced
- 1 tablespoon lemon juice

Method:

1. Add all ingredients to a blender.
2. Blend until smooth.
3. Refrigerate for up to 1 day.

Nutritional Content:

- Calories: 143.5
- Fat: 1.1 g
- Cholesterol: 0 mg
- Sodium: 81 mg
- Carbohydrates: 36 g
- Fiber: 7.7 g
- Sugar: 12 g
- Protein: 4.2 g

Watermelon Water

Preparation Time: 20 minutes
Cooking Time: 0 minute
Servings: 4

Ingredients:

- 4 cups watermelon, sliced into cubes
- 8 cups water
- 4 lime slices
- 1/8 cup mint leaves

Method:

1. Blend watermelon in a food processor.
2. Add to a pitcher with water along with lime slices and mint leaves.
3. Refrigerate for up to 3 days.

Nutritional Content:

- Calories: 25
- Fat: 0.1 g
- Cholesterol: 0 mg
- Sodium: 1.3 mg
- Carbohydrates: 18 g
- Fiber: 0.4 g
- Sugar: 17 g
- Protein: 0.5 g

Blueberry Smoothie

Preparation Time: 5 minutes
Cooking Time: 0 minute
Servings: 2

Ingredients:

- 1 cup blueberries
- 8 oz. yogurt
- ¾ cup nonfat milk
- 2 tablespoons Splenda
- ½ teaspoon vanilla extract
- ⅛ teaspoon ground nutmeg

Method:

1. Combine all ingredients in a blender.
2. Pulse until smooth.
3. Transfer to a pitcher
4. Refrigerate for up to 1 day.

Nutritional Content:

- Calories: 211
- Fat: 9.5 g
- Cholesterol: 0 mg
- Sodium: 17 mg
- Carbohydrates: 24 g
- Fiber: 1.8 g
- Sugar: 3 g
- Protein: 9.5 g

Chapter 11: 4-Weekly Meal Plan

Week 1

Sunday

Breakfast: Cottage cheese pancake

Lunch: Pureed carrot

Dinner: Zucchini soup with rosemary

Monday

Breakfast: Baked eggs with broccoli

Lunch: Pumpkin puree

Dinner: Chicken tikka masala

Tuesday

Breakfast: Breakfast popsicle

Lunch: Cream of asparagus soup

Dinner: Tofu & quinoa bowl

Wednesday

Breakfast: Pumpkin oatmeal

Lunch: Roasted sweet potato puree

Dinner: Crispy chicken

Thursday

Breakfast: Breakfast strawberry wrap

Lunch: Ginger beef stir fry

Dinner: Mushroom soup

Friday

Breakfast: Baked eggs with broccoli

Lunch: Mashed parsnips

Dinner: Creamy chicken

Saturday

Breakfast: Baked spinach & cottage cheese

Lunch: Celery root puree

Dinner: Cajun chicken

Week 2

Sunday

Breakfast: Breakfast enchilada

Lunch: Baked chicken & vegetables

Dinner: Hummus

Monday

Breakfast: Pumpkin oatmeal

Lunch: Creamy acorn squash soup

Dinner: Tofu & quinoa bowl

Tuesday

Breakfast: Breakfast sandwich

Lunch: Roasted sweet potato puree

Dinner: Chicken tikka masala

Wednesday

Breakfast: Broccoli & tofu scramble

Lunch: Kale soup with white beans

Dinner: Asian-style pork tenderloin

Thursday

Breakfast: Cottage cheese pancake

Lunch: Crispy tuna patties

Dinner: Tomato soup

Week 3

Sunday

Breakfast: Breakfast enchilada

Lunch: Tofu & quinoa bowl

Dinner: Fried trout

Monday

Breakfast: Baked spinach & cottage cheese

Lunch: Butternut squash & coconut milk soup

Dinner: Pork & black bean stew

Tuesday

Breakfast: Cottage cheese pancake

Lunch: Barbecue salmon

Dinner: Chicken & broccoli soup

Wednesday

Breakfast: Breakfast sandwich

Friday

Breakfast: Egg muffin

Lunch: Creamy chicken

Dinner: Ginger beef stir fry

Saturday

Breakfast: Breakfast popsicle

Lunch: Chicken casserole

Dinner: Mushroom soup

Lunch: Chicken casserole

Dinner: Tomato soup

Thursday

Breakfast: Breakfast popsicle

Lunch: Broccoli puree

Dinner: Greek chicken

Friday

Breakfast: Broccoli & tofu scramble

Lunch: Crispy tuna patties

Dinner: Potato soup

Saturday

Breakfast: Egg muffin

Lunch: Chicken & broccoli soup

Dinner: Fried trout

Week 4

Sunday

Breakfast: Breakfast strawberry wrap

Lunch: Barbecue salmon

Dinner: Butternut squash & coconut milk soup

Monday

Breakfast: Breakfast sandwich

Lunch: Greek chicken

Dinner: Potato soup

Tuesday

Breakfast: Breakfast enchilada

Lunch: Sweet & sour pork

Dinner: Creamy cauliflower puree

Wednesday

Breakfast: Baked eggs with broccoli

Lunch: Chicken casserole

Dinner: Pureed carrot

Thursday

Breakfast: Baked spinach & cottage cheese

Lunch: Broccoli puree

Dinner: Fried trout

Friday

Breakfast: Egg muffin

Lunch: Crispy tuna patties

Dinner: Carrot & parsnip puree

Saturday

Breakfast: Pumpkin oatmeal

Lunch: Creamy cauliflower puree

Dinner: Pork & black bean stew

Conclusion

If you suffer from IBS or any other digestive symptoms, such as gas, bloating, and pain. These intestine issues may be due to irritable bowel disease (IBD), Diverticulitis, Small intestine Bacteria overgrowth (SIBO). The book includes a low-Fodmap eating plan that explains in detail which foods are not allowed and why.

Thank you for buying this book. Now let's start your gourmet journey! Nourish and protect your gut with these diverse and delightful dishes!

www.ingramcontent.com/pod-product-compliance
Lightning Source LLC
Chambersburg PA
CBHW081404070526
44583CB00020B/2666